Friendship is a gift,
continually giving happiness.
It is strong and supportive,
and few things in all the world
will ever compare with the joy
that comes from its wonderful bond.

— Mia Evans

ACKNOWLEDGMENTS appear on page 48.

Library of Congress Catalog Card Number: 98-16824
ISBN: 0-88396-465-1

Registered in the U.S. Patent and Trademark Office.
Certain trademarks are used under license.

Manufactured in the United States of America
Fourth Printing: April 2000

This book is printed on recycled paper.

Library of Congress Cataloging-in-Publication Data

Friends for life : a collection of poems / edited by Gary Morris.
p. cm.
ISBN 0-88396-465-1 (alk. paper)
1. Friendship--Poetry. 2. American poetry--20th century.
I. Morris, Gary, 1958- .
PS595.F75F76 1998
811' .54080353--dc21 98-16824
CIP

Friends for Life

A collection of poems
Edited by Gary Morris

SPS Studios, Inc.
Boulder, Colorado

Friends for Life

When two people
have shared
as much as you and I have;
when they've opened up
their hearts,
shared their dreams,
thoughts, and fears;
when two people
know each other well enough
to know if sadness
is hiding behind a smile
or if happiness is
glowing in the eyes;
when they've shared
so many laughs,
and when each other's pain
at times has triggered tears;
when two people
believe in one another
and are always sincere
to each other;
when they
have trusted one another
with the truth
that lies within —
then you can be sure
that they're friends for life...
just like
you and me.

— Zoe Dellous

True Friendship Has Many Ingredients

True friendship isn't seen
with the eyes;
it's felt with the heart
when there is trust,
understanding, secrets,
loyalty, and sharing.
Friendship is a feeling
rarely found in life,
but when it is found
it has a profound impact
on one's well-being,
strength, and character.

A true friendship does not need
elaborate gifts
or spectacular events
in order to be valuable or valued.
To ensure long-lasting quality
and satisfaction,
a friendship only needs
certain key ingredients:
undying loyalty,
unmatched understanding,
unsurpassed trust,
deep and soulful secrets,
and endless sharing.
These ingredients, mixed with
personality and a sense of humor,
can make friendship
last a lifetime.

— Sonya Williams

There Are Some Friends We Hold Close to Our Hearts

As we walk our path of life,
we meet people every day.
Most are simply met by chance,
but some are sent our way.
These become the special friends
whose bond we can't explain —
the ones who understand us
and share our joy and pain.
Their love contains no boundaries,
so even when apart,
their presence still embraces us
with a warmth felt in the heart.
This love becomes a passageway
where even miles disappear.
And so these friends life sends our way
remain forever near.

— Lisa Pelzer Vetter

Our Friendship Is a Miracle

When two people join together as friends, it is truly one of life's greatest gifts. Friends stand beside each other, not in front or behind. They are two people joined in the soul, transcending all known bonds and life's limitations.

We each have a different path to walk in life, and sometimes our lives become burdens we must bear.

Friends help to ease the burden and give us comfort — not through lofty speeches and glamorous words, but simply by their presence.

As miracles, friendships don't happen every day. They are hard to find and even harder to keep. But when we find someone special in our lives, our journey through time becomes easier.

You and I have been blessed by the gift of friendship. Many things in our lives may come and go; some are as fleeting as sand castles on the shore. But like the ocean, our friendship is the foundation and root of who we are and who we must be.

May you and I remain forever united by the simple act of knowing what it means to give of ourselves to each other, and by the peace that comes from knowing we are friends.

— Sharon Whyte

A Best Friend...

Someone who is concerned with
everything you do ❧ someone to
call upon during good and bad
times ❧ someone who understands
whatever you do ❧ someone who
tells you the truth about yourself ❧
someone who knows what you are
going through at all times ❧
someone who does not compete
with you ❧ someone who is
genuinely happy for you when things
go well ❧ someone who tries to
cheer you up when things don't
go well ❧ someone who is an
extension of yourself without which
you are not complete ❧
My best friend is you

— Susan Polis Schutz

Friendship, Forever and Ever

I want you to know: I am really happy to have the kind of friendship I have with you. I love it because it's true and real and trusting. Because it does my heart and soul good to know that I'm going to be here for you... and you for me... when there are needs that need to be tended to, when there are feelings that need to be felt, and when there are smiles that simply need to be shared in the company of someone who really cares.

I don't know if I could ever completely describe to you how important our friendship is to me. But it is so much a part of all that is good in my world.

Sometimes you feel like a gift that was given to my days to make sure that they would always have some happiness in them. More than once, I have felt that what I lack in life, I make up for by having a friendship that I wouldn't trade for anything. Anytime. Anywhere.

I have dreams in my life that may never come true, travels I may never take, goals I may not be able to reach, and hopes that might always be just beyond my horizons. But I want you to know that whether my wishes come true or whether they disappear altogether, I will always feel like one of the luckiest people in the world.

Because I have a friend — in you. And because we're going to be friends — forever.

— Jordan Carrill

My Friend,
This Is to Thank You...

For all those times when I never could
have managed without a friend like you.

For being such a constant in my life —
amidst all the changes
the rest of my world goes through.

For being remarkable in your qualities,
inspiring in your thoughts,
and caring in your heart.

For being the one I will always feel close to,
whether we're together or miles apart.

For being my definition of "special,"
and for proving it over and
over again.

And for all the times
I never told you before...

I thank you
so dearly,
my friend.

— Casey Whilson

My Hopes for Our Friendship

I hope our friendship can be a source of comfort to you
...like a blanket to wrap around you
when you're cold
...like a pillow for you to use to rest your head
...like arms to hold you when you're weary
and feeling alone
...like a handkerchief to catch your tears

I hope our friendship can be a source of
strength to you
...like sunshine when you need warmth in
your life
...like music that soothes your emptiness
and fills a lonely space
...like a meal when you're hungry
and want to eat
...like a shoulder when you need something
to lean on

I hope our friendship can be a source of
love to you
...like someone who offers praise
and never pressure
...like someone who is there to talk to
when you need to talk
...like someone who is there for you to be
whatever it is you need
...like someone who loves you
just the way you are

I hope our friendship can be a source of
certainty for you that you always have
someone on your side
...to give you hope that there is a way
through everything
...to give you confidence that there is
a light at the end of the tunnel
...to be a voice that says, "Congratulations!
You've made it through another one!"
...to share with you every challenge,
every joy, every trial in your life.

— Donna Fargo

The Time We Spend Together Means Everything to Me

One quality of our relationship
that I deeply cherish
is our natural ability
to enjoy and appreciate
the time we have
to spend with one another.

When you are present,
the fun and happy moments
come so freely,
because we are never trying
to force an emotion.

When you are absent,
I cannot help but miss you,
yet the quality
of our time spent together
leaves me feeling
warm, happy, and content.

For all the times we have,
please continue to be yourself,
because that is the person
I admire, respect, and love,
for yesterday, today, and tomorrow.

— Scott McCormish

Friends don't always need
a lot of words to stay close.
There's a silent communication
always taking place within
their minds and hearts.
They communicate much
while speaking few words.
They sense within their spirits
when the other is in need.
They know when to reach out
and when to stay away.
They know when to speak out
and when to remain silent.
Friends, no matter how far apart they are,
can stay close with few words,
as long as there is love in their hearts
for each other.

— Sherrie L. Householder

Old Friends Are Always the Ones You Cherish Most

There is nothing like an old friend.
With old friends, the only requirement
is that you be yourself.
You can say whatever is on your mind
and do whatever you feel like doing.
You never have to worry because
you know your friendship is not based
on perfection, but on respect
and acceptance.

With old friends,
you can share the most intimate
and important aspects of yourself,
knowing that their beauty and value
will be recognized and appreciated.

With old friends,
distance has no meaning or power.
There's a bridge made of
love and memories,
joys and sorrows,
that connects old friends
and keeps them close.

With old friends, you feel safe.
They've been there for you
through the roughest storms,
so you know you can trust them,
believe in them, and count on them.
You know they will be at your side,
so there is peace within your heart.

With old friends, you never feel lonely
because the roots that bind you
have grown deep and strong.
Your friendship has withstood
the test of time.

— Nancye Sims

Our Friendship Means the World to Me

We've discussed so openly
the many personal aspects
of our lives.
We've talked about our needs,
our dreams,
our similarities and differences.
We've given one another
the freedom to ask anything
and talk about everything.
We've put all of our concerns
in the open,
so that we'd have the freedom
to grow and be ourselves.
You've been a ray of hope
and my source of laughter
when I wanted to cry.

You've touched me
with just a word of encouragement
when I was down.
You've been my shelter
when times were tough.
You stayed here beside me,
offering hope and showering me
with your love.

You've been the one person
I can tell anything to,
no matter how personal
or how much it might hurt.
You haven't judged me
based on my past.
We've never held one another down;
we've respected each other,
and we've laughed.

These are just a few of
the reasons why
our friendship means
the world to me.
It's the most precious gift
I could ever receive.

— Sherrie L. Householder

Remember Me When You Need a Friend

Remember me when you feel
lost or lonely.
I will always be your loyal friend.
You will not need to look far
to find me,
because I will always
meet you halfway.
Remember me when you think
of the people who care
the most about you.

Remember me if you need
someone to talk to.
I will always listen to you
attentively
and support you wholeheartedly.
When you experience
a joyful occasion in your life,
be sure to invite me
to share your happiness with you.
When you have no one else to turn to,
I will always be here for you
and do whatever I can to help.
Remember me and the wonderful
friendship that we share,
and always take comfort
in the fact that you
are special in my eyes.

— Kelly D. Caron

You know when someone special
touches your life...
   They always know just the right
      thing to say or do;
   They can make you feel better
      just by being near;
   They listen with an open heart
      and understand;
   They laugh with you when you're happy;
   They share your tears when you're sad;
   They are there beside you
      whenever you feel alone;
   They extend their hand when
      you need support;
   They are proud of all that
      you accomplish;
   They love you just because you're you.

You know when someone special
   touches your life...
And my life was touched
   the day that I met you.

— Geri Danks

You Are One in a Million!

There is a handful of people
in this cold world
who can warm the hearts of others.

Their happiness is genuine,
their smiles are sincere,
and their love
shows in their actions.

There is a handful of people
in this world
who can light the way at midnight.
They can dry tears with a smile.
Their hearts are open,
and they always have room
for one more person in their lives.

At first glance
they appear to be like everyone else,
but a second look reveals an
extraordinary person.

There is a handful of people
in this cold world
who can warm the hearts of others.

Thank you
for being one of those people.

— Susan M. Tyrrell

I Will Never Forget You or the Times That We Have Shared

The laughter we shared in happy times
and the tears in sad ones
will all be tucked away
in my heart
behind a door marked "Good Memories."
On quiet days of remembrance,
I will remove these thoughts
one by one
and I will think of you
with a happy sadness in my soul.
Though miles and months
may come between us,
you will still be my friend
and I will be yours —
always eager to hear from you
and share your life again.

— Melissa Haynes Chaffin

Where there is friendship,
There can be no loneliness;
How sad can we be
in the presence of a friend?

Where there is friendship,
There can be no poverty;
How poor can we be
when we have a friend
to share our day?

Where there is friendship,
There can be no failure;
How defeated can we be
when we have a friend
to encourage and comfort our heart?

Where there is friendship,
There is hope for the future.
How hopeless can we feel
when we have a friend
who stands by us and sees
our true potential?

Friendship is the gift of sunshine
on a cloudy day,
A helping hand that makes us
laugh our cares away
And brings us courage to face another day.

Thank you for always
being there for me;
Thank you for being my friend.

— Susanne B. Simmons

Promise Me That You Will...

Be kind to yourself.
Look in the mirror and see
that you are beautiful.
Make three wishes.
Be strong.
Nurture your soul.
Continue your prayers.
Let go of any pain.
Banish any anger.
Take one moment at a time.
Hear music.
Make music.
Seek inspiration.
Learn.

Promise me that you will...

Believe in fairy tales
and in the magic
of your dreams.
Find that dreams do come true.
Hug yourself.
Feel the sun shine.
Believe again.
Smile.
Seek laughter.
Always remember that you have
a guardian angel
watching over you.
Find hope.
Find your true love.

Promise me these things.

— Linda Ann McConnell

The Heart of Friendship

In the heart of friendship
we find serenity,
a place of peace,
and unconditional love.
We soon discover that
differences don't matter,
because what's important is
the opportunity to share.

In the heart of friendship,
we find ourselves connected
to an endless source
of understanding
from someone who will listen
and be there with support.

We find that time goes better,
more fun is involved,
thoughts and feelings are expressed,
plans are shared,
and hopes and dreams gain
much encouragement.

And we come to know that
it doesn't really matter
if the skies above are ever
blue or grey —
for as long as friends
are spending time together,
the world will always be
a bright and shining place.

— Barbara J. Hall

The Importance of Friendship

In all facets of life,
it is important to have someone
to trust and confide in
with your hopes, dreams,
and times of struggle.
Friends understand and listen.
They let you know that
you are not alone and that
the moments you share are some
of the best parts of life.

— Ben Daniels

Friendship is sunshine on a cloudy day,
the rainbow that follows the storm,
gentle ripples on a peaceful pond,
a heart that always holds you close.
Friendship is that intimate place
where you can always safely go.

— Judith J. Yerman

Friendship is a responsibility.
When your life touches another's,
you become responsible for the way
you affect that person's feelings.
Friendship means setting aside
your own troubles and feelings
to take the time to listen.
It means helping whenever possible,
even if it's an inconvenience
or a burden to you.
Friendship requires strength,
patience, and understanding.
But more than anything else,
it requires love.

— Jeanne Radke

The Friendship Creed

If you can't be everything to somebody, reach out and just be a friend. If you can't be somebody's whole life, be satisfied with making their moment or their day. Give them a smile and a gesture of friendship to warm them. Do something nice for them, something unexpected. People appreciate even the smallest offer of kindness and acceptance — a call, a note, or whatever you decide... that will do.

If you can't solve somebody's problems, just make them feel a little better about something. Make them feel good about themselves. It doesn't have to be a big deal or cost a lot of money. It can just be something thoughtful and small. Let them know that someone is thinking of them. Make their world a little better, even for a short while. They just might need a lift, you never know. Don't hold back. Life is too short. Don't wait. They might need you. If you can't make their day, then brighten a moment for them. It could be important.

— Donna Fargo

What I Wish for You, My Friend...

I wish you blue skies and a peaceful heart... a long and happy life... confidence to listen to the voice that speaks to you from within... courage to follow your dreams... understanding for the times when you stray from your path... the chance to be everything you want to be... whatever material and intangible wealth you need... work that is fulfilling and satisfying... permission to forgive yourself if you should ever fall short of your goals... that your greatest success in life will come at a time that is most meaningful for you...

I wish for you, my friend... a place
where you can live in harmony with
nature and the rest of the world...
magical nights... fun and excitement
each day... serenity... people who care
deeply about you... and whom you
care about, too... memories of times
and places that will always remain
close to your heart... wishes made on
stars that eventually come true...
knowledge of what a dear and
exceptional friend you are to me...
that all these special wishes will
someday unfold for you.

— Anna Marie Edwards

For a Very Special Friend

There are so many things
to do each day
There is so much going on in the world
of great concern
that often we do not stop and think about
what is really important to us
One of the nicest things in my life
is my friendship with you
and even if we don't have a lot of time
to spend with each other
I want you to always know
how much I appreciate you
and our friendship

— Susan Polis Schutz

Friends

Friends are very special people who accept
each other with an unconditional caring. They

Recognize each other's talents and faults and
acknowledge them without judgment.

They are Incapable of turning away when times
are tough and life's problems seem hard to bear.

Instead, they Encourage each other so they can
enjoy the good times and find strength to endure the

bad times. They're Never afraid to say what
they feel and can be honest without causing

hurt or pain. They can Depend on each other
because they have the kind of trust

that allows them to Share the best and worst
of their lives with laughter and without fear.

You are one of these special people,
and I'm glad you are my friend.

— Andrea L. Hines

There Will Always Be a Place in My Heart for You

Inside of me there is a place... where my
sweetest dreams reside ❧ where my highest
hopes are kept alive ❧ where my deepest
feelings are felt ❧ and where my favorite
memories are tucked away, safe and warm ❧
My heart is a lasting source of happiness ❧
Only the most special things in my world get
to come inside and stay there forever ❧

And every time I get in touch with
the hopes, feelings, and memories
in my heart, I realize how deeply
my life has been touched
by you ❧

— Emilia Larson

Friendship

Friendship begins with meeting someone along the path of life. Someone you get to know, and gradually get to know even better. You discover what a joy it is to spend your moments with this person. It's nice the way the good feelings remain. The happiness lasts, and the memories you make start to turn into some of your favorite treasures. Friendship is two paths converging on the way to the same beautiful view.

Friendship is walking
the way together...

Friendship is opening up to one another. Sharing thoughts and feelings in a way that never felt very comfortable before. It is a complete trust, sweetened with a lot more understanding and communication than many people will ever know. Friendship is two hearts that share and which are able to say things no outsiders ever could. Friendship is an inner door that only a friend has the key to. Friendship is a gift, continually giving happiness. It is strong and supportive, and few things in all the world will ever compare with the joy that comes from its wonderful bond.

I want you to know that our friendship is one thing I'll cherish all my life, and it's something that you can always count on.

— Mia Evans

ACKNOWLEDGMENTS

The following is a partial list of authors whom the publisher especially wishes to thank for permission to reprint their works.

PrimaDonna Entertainment Corp. for "My Hopes for Our Friendship" and "The Friendship Creed," by Donna Fargo. Copyright © 1998 by PrimaDonna Entertainment Corp. All rights reserved. Reprinted by permission.

Geri Danks for "You know when someone special touches your life..." Copyright © 1998 by Geri Danks. All rights reserved. Reprinted by permission.

Melissa Haynes Chaffin for "I Will Never Forget You or the Times That We Have Shared." Copyright © 1998 by Melissa Haynes Chaffin. All rights reserved. Reprinted by permission.

Susanne B. Simmons for "Where there is friendship..." Copyright © 1998 by Susanne B. Simmons. All rights reserved. Reprinted by permission.

Linda Ann McConnell for "Promise Me That You Will..." Copyright © 1998 by Linda Ann McConnell. All rights reserved. Reprinted by permission.

Barbara J. Hall for "The Heart of Friendship." Copyright © 1998 by Barbara j. Hall. All rights reserved. Reprinted by permission.

A careful effort has been made to trace the ownership of poems used in this anthology in order to obtain permission to reprint copyrighted materials and give proper credit to the copyright owners. If any error or omission has occurred, it is completely inadvertent, and we would like to make corrections in future editions provided that written notification is made to the publisher: SPS STUDIOS, INC., P.O. Box 4549, Boulder, Colorado 80306.